EPIC RITES PRESS

doing cartwheels on doomsday afternoon

poetry by John Yamrus

First edition. Printed in Canada.

Editors: Wolfgang Carstens and David McLean
Interior: Wolfgang Carstens
Exterior: Pablo Vision

ISBN 978-0-9811844-8-7

epic rites press publications are available through www.epicrites.org, as well as through our distributor, SPD (Small Press Distribution) and may be ordered online at www.spdbooks.org and/or by addressing:

Small Press Distribution, 1341 Seventh Street, Berkeley, CA, 94710-1409. Phone 510.524.1668 or 800.869.7553 (Toll-free within the US). E-mail spd@spdbooks.org.

For Kathy

acknowledgments

Some of these poems have appeared in the following publications: St. Vitus Press, The Orange Room Review, Outlaw Poetry, Metropolis, Sacramento Poetry, Short Story Library, The Exuberant Ashtray, Epic Rites Journal and Chiron Review. If any publication was skipped, please understand that it was unintentional.

Contents

introduction by Rob Plath

John Yamrus, as a poet, is like an expert skeet shooter that hits the clay pigeon no matter what the speed, angle or trajectory; in poem after poem, his sharp mind nails its target every time. This is a difficult task too because John's subject matter is constantly changing, unlike the woman he speaks of in the poem on page 31,

she cursed like a

sailor.
it was in her
poetry,
it was
in
her speech, it
was in her
letters.
it was like
this crutch
that colored
everything
she
did.

i
never liked

that.

John Yamrus' poems contain no crutches unless you want
to call candor and clarity crutches. But that would be just
plain stupidity. Speaking of clarity, in the poem that
follows on page 32, he describes a frustrated delusional
hack,

the failed poet

talks
a good game.

she says
her poems
are only about
positive things…
encouraging people…

uplifting them.

she says
anything else
is a waste
of god's
gift.

personally,
i like my poems

with a bit more grit
and guts.

i tend to
see the dirt
before the sky.

John, unlike the failed poet or any other wannabe, is
disillusioned. You have to be disillusioned to tell the truth
in this existence. All his poems are the work of a realist, a
seasoned veteran of the poetry field. When he says he sees
"dirt" before "sky," this isn't just meaningless morbidity
but the vision of someone anchored in truth, the concrete,
the ground we walk upon. He tells us no lies because he
doesn't lie to himself. This takes guts in this life, especially
in these times; in the age of deception, candor is a crime.
John Yamrus is one of the few warriors out there telling it
like it is. In the short poem on page 36 he sums it up quite
simply,

if

you ask
for my opinion

don't
get pissed
when i

give
it.

One recurrent subject I noticed in John's poems, subtle or
obvious, is endurance. Bukowski once said, "Endurance is
more important than truth." Aren't both equally important,
though? Maybe old Hank was just being an ass at the time
he said that. I think John's work is testament that endurance
and truth are a double yoke. He's been writing since 1970
and has 19 books published, he's endured year after year
after year of the struggle to create, all while telling the
truth. Here's one of my favorites in the book on endurance,

i've got

this hair
on my nose,

near
the tip,

and
no matter
how often

i
cut it,

or

pluck it,

it keeps
coming back.

now,
that's just

damned
admirable…

don't you think?

I admire John Yamrus. His candor, his clarity, and his
endurance. He's one of the few damned admirable ones out
there. You'll see as you read this book.

Cheers, John.

- Rob Plath (author of A Bellyful of Anarchy - epic rites
press 2009)

December 2009

doing cartwheels on doomsday afternoon

poetry by John Yamrus

Eddie

liked to
think he was
stronger than dirt,

but
he had a
weak spot
in his heart
for his dog,
Bastard.

now,
old Bastard,
he was tough.

he'd been hit
by cars
twice,

and,
even when Eddie
found him,

three years ago,
under the Parker's steps,

with a

broken leg
and his throat cut,

he didn't even
whimper.

Eddie wouldn't have
noticed him

if he
didn't hear him
moving around
in the leaves.

in fact,
that's how
the dog
got his name.

when Eddie saw
the condition he was in,
he said
"Bastard!"
and the dog
just looked at him,
as if to say
"back at ya, buddy!"
they were tight

since then,
Eddie and the Bastard.

he liked to think
they'd be
friends forever,

but, he knew
it didn't
work that way.

one day
the old Bastard
would run out of luck…

a car would
get him
and that'd be
the end of it.

that was fine,
with Eddie.

nothing
lasts
forever.
until that time,
they'd just
hang out,

him
and the Bastard.

besides,
what they've got
is ten times
better

than
immortality.

this morning

i was
nearly killed

by a
car

speeding through
the parking lot
at the
liquor store.

how

perfectly

fitting.

Randolph was an ass...

he
didn't know it,

but he was an ass
all the same.

he loved to
argue.

he'd argue
about anything.

i'd call it
red,
he'd call it
black.

no matter
what i'd say,
it was wrong,

and he had
the better
idea.

i can't say
he didn't make

perfect sense
every now
and then.

there was that time
i came to him
and said
"man, this is
a great day,
isn't it?
look at
that sky.
you just gotta
smile."

and he turned to me,
like he always did,
with that
shit eating grin
and said:

"sure,
you're happy now,

but,
don't worry,
you'll
get over it."

he thought it was

the height of wit
to say:

"walkin' on water
ain't no
miracle

if
the lake's
froze over."

that was fine
the first
time,

but,
he often
said it

twice
a day.

every
day.

for
two years.

finally,
i had
enough.

i
said to him:

"just once,
can't you
come up with
something else?"

he
smiled

and said

"god just
don't like ugly,
does he?"

and
went back
to his work.

if pressed,
i'd have to say
that he's
the

only
reason

i
won't have
anything to do

with
lakes.

she cursed like a

sailor.
it was in her
poetry,
it was
in
her speech, it
was in her
letters.
it was like
this crutch
that colored
everything
she
did.

i
never liked
that.

the failed poet

talks
a good game.

she says
her poems
are only about
positive things…

encouraging people…

uplifting them.

she says
anything else
is a waste
of god's
gift.

personally,
i like my poems
with a bit more grit
and guts.

i tend to
see the dirt
before the sky.

that's all
well and good…

there's
room enough here
for both of us
to be wrong.

but,
the thing that kills me
is
that
she refuses
to look at her work
critically.

it came from god…
then it must be perfect,
right?

i hate to tell her
it doesn't always
work that way.

i
point her out
because i know
she can't

cut it.

and i know
i can.

and
that's just
stupid

and arrogant…

but, also
true.

besides,
calling yourself

a
poet

won't
necessarily
make you one.

just like
me
calling myself
an ass
doesn't

NOT
make me one,

does it?

if

you ask
for my opinion

don't
get pissed

when i
give
it.

i've got

this hair
on my nose,

near
the tip,

and
no matter
how often

i
cut it,

or
pluck it,

it keeps
coming back.

now,
that's just

damned
admirable...

don't you think?

he's in his 60's

in a
wheelchair.

his wife
cuts the grass,
drives the car,
feeds him,
cleans him and
everything else.

sometimes
the gods are good to you…

sometimes
they're not.

you just never know…

and so
you play the hand
you're dealt,

whether it's
a wheelchair
or a pot of
gold.
and if you're lucky

you end up
twisted and
bent,

with a damn
fine woman
who fights back
the blood-curdling screams
and just

endures.

the miracle

is
not
always

what it
appears
to be.

the
miracle
sometimes

is
only
smoke

and
mirrors

and
some poor slob's
picture

of his
slightly
broken
dreams.

they tell me

i'm writing too much
about writing
lately.

in fact,
they tell me
a lot of
things.

"you're a fraud,"
they say,
"these aren't
poems,

these
are just
diary entries.

what are you
trying
to do,

pull a fast one?"

what i should say
is
i haven't

pulled a fast one
in years,

but
i don't.

i let it
go.

just
like i let
all the other
comments
go.

see this
poem?

consider it
my one
and only

fast
one

pulled
today.

Tommy was a duker...

he'd fight with
any one,
any where
any time.

it
didn't matter
to Tommy.

one time,
when he was
still in high school,
i saw him
take on
3 college guys.

they
never even
had a chance.

yesterday,
i heard
Tommy was
dead.

cancer.
i guess

he finally
learned

you just
can't

win 'em
all.

he smelled

of
coffee,

and
cigarettes…

of
cheap liquor,

and
cheaper women.

he
liked to sleep

with
his window open.

the
snippets of talk

sounded
like poetry to him.

"of
course, i can't…"

"but,

maybe i should…"

"it's
all a cheat…"

he'd
lie there, thinking

you're
totally right…

about
all of it.

my dog doesn't care much

for
literature.
she doesn't care
that the editors write
asking questions,
demanding
answers.

she doesn't
care
that
there's
books to be sold,

poems
to be written,

and
hands to
shake.

all she wants
is to have
her bowl
filled

her

head
scratched

and
to be
let out
when it's
time to
shit.

i just now

agreed to
an interview.

this one's
for monday.

it'll be
the same old questions,

like:

"how'd you get
started?"

"who
do you read?"

and
"who are you influenced by?"

all the same questions
and never once
do i get asked
the right
one.

in my
opinion,

the only one.

the one that
says:

"you write a lot about
dogs…

why is that?"

if they'd only
ask me
that

i'd go away
happy.

i'd sit them down
and tell them

exactly

what the dogs
do for me…

they teach me
joy,

perseverance

and
acceptance.

they teach me
total concentration
on a single task.

and
most of all
they teach me
the secret...

the answer to
the one question
i'm asked the most.

the one question
that i'll never
answer.

they wouldn't
believe me
even if i
did.

they'd think
i'm lying.

but, you won't,

will you?

the truth
is

the great secret
these dogs
teach me

is
there isn't
any.

the next question

he asked
was the usual:

"so,
who's had
the most influence
on your poetry?"

i looked at him
and said:

"Hank Williams,
Groucho Marx
and Willie Mays."

i've heard it said
the pleasures of the damned
are few
and far between.

this
was one of mine.

we were at

the hotel bar,
ordering drinks.

i got
tequila for me
and she wanted
something pink,

so, i asked for
a strawberry colada.

the waitress looks at me
and says
"we don't serve
daiquiris."

i looked at her
and ordered
a wine
instead.

there was live music
at the bar...

the Jerry Stein Trio.

there were

two of them.

right then
they were playing
the old Patsy Cline hit
"Crazy."

they were playing it
real slow,

and
it was kinda nice.

maybe it was
the tequila…

but it was nice.

one of the guys
at the bar,
who hadn't said a word
all night,
turned to me
and said
"they're playing
an Eagles song.

i
love

the Eagles.

that's Desperado.

i know that damn song
by heart."

that's just the kind
of night it was.

nothing seemed to fit.

some nights
are like that.

some nights you just
lower your head,

deal
with it

and take
one

for
the team.

if

you're not
where

you want
to be,

you may be
where

you ought
to be.

when i was a kid, i

worked in a
shoe factory.

i was a
"heeler,"

putting heels on
women's shoes.

i'd glue the heels
to the soles

and put them on
a conveyor
that took them to a
"trimmer"
who sanded the excess.

if i didn't
do it
well enough,

or
fast enough,

he'd turn around
and throw a shoe

at me.

pretty soon,
it got to be a
routine.

i'd glue
and duck, and
glue and
duck.

i was
young and
quick…

he rarely ever
hit me.

eventually,
the work ran out,

and i
moved on.

i often wondered
what drives a
man
to act like that?

after all,
we were
piece workers.

we got paid
by the shoe.

it cost him money
to throw
at me.

anyway,
that was a long,
long
time ago,

and
i'm sure he's
dead by now.

Leo…

his name
was
Leo.

Mackley leans over

and says to me:
"listen to that,
will ya?

did you ever notice
how every country song
on the radio
sounds like
George Strait?

like this one,
for instance...

it's
George Strait."

i look at him and say:
"but that's
a woman
singing."

"doesn't matter...

George Strait.

every freakin' song
on the radio...

it's
George Strait."

he sat there,
listening for a bit,
and said

"god, i hate
country music,
don't you?"

"damn straight."

they're winning, you know...

their forced,
fake,
academic poetry
is slowly winning the day...

not because it's better...

because
it's safe.

it gives them a formula
to work with...

a rack
to hang their
thoughtless
thoughts on.

there was a time,
once,
when i thought
i'd manage
to pull them over
to the dark side,

but they wouldn't
take the bait.

they're
smarter than i thought.

now,
i continue
to work the poems,

sticking my head up
every now and then,
to take
a pot shot.

and,
i notice
the battle's
not over yet...
there's still a few of us left.

one there...
another, over there...

enough to
put up a fight.

enough
to continue
this beautiful,
monstrous thing.

reality check...

i had just
picked up the mail
and found that it contained
a check and a statement
from one of my publishers.

more than a little
pleased with myself,
i took it in to my wife
who was watching her soaps on tv.

she looked at the check...

looked at me...

then turned back to her soaps
and said:

"whatever you do, buddy,
don't quit your day job."

she's ashamed

of
my books.

i
never
knew it

until
a minute ago.

i'd called to
ask her
if
i sent her
an extra copy
of my newest,

would she give it
to these friends of hers…

people
i recently met.

they were nice,
retired,

and i felt like

giving them a gift.

anyway,
when i asked if
she'd give them the book
she said "honestly?"

and
paused.

i knew
why

and said
"what's the matter?
would you be ashamed?"

"i would."

"that's fine," i said.
"don't worry
about it."

when i was a kid,
during frequent
absences from school,

with
chicken pox,

the measles
or the mumps,

i used to lie in bed,
on a self-proclaimed mission
to read the dictionary,
front to back…

all
1,241 pages of it.

when she got home
from school,
she used to
bring me soup,

and
talk to me,

and
sit with me.

in part,
due to her,
i now know
that abashment,
mortification,
ignominy
and reproach

are just
four other words

for
shame.

"write a poem about THAT,"

she
said,

sitting
on the edge
of the bed,

smiling.

she said

"you stink,
i can't stand
to even look at you.

every time you
lay hands on me
my skin crawls.

eat shit
and die
you bastard."

as she left the room
she didn't hear him say
"i hear THAT, darlin',

i sure hear that."

a word to the wise:

never
be afraid

to
piss off
your readers.

when
you start
worrying about
what they
think,

then you
might as well
pack it
in.

giving

them
what they
want

can
be hard

on
a man's

soul.

the publisher

wanted
to put out a book
of mine
and he wanted
it
to be out by
a certain date
and i didn't
have
enough
poems
to fill it
up
so i
panicked
and walked
the streets
looking
for something
to happen
waiting
for someone to
say something
interesting
and it

just wasn't
happening
so i
figured
i'd have to
take the
bull by the
horns
and do it
myself
and
i thought i'd
take
a cue
from Bob
Dylan
so
i
built a
fire on
Main Street
and
shot it
full of
holes.

seriously,

this
whole
poetry thing
is not
that
com
plicated.

you
say
exactly
what
you
have
to say,

then
sit
on
the
couch

and
watch
American Idol.

they're like that on the net

on those
poetry sites

they all
have names

like
Musegal

and
PoeMan

and
Rhymer,

announcing
who
or what
they think
they are.

i really
don't think
they're doing it
for security.

i think

they're
ashamed.

deep down
inside

they know.

and they don't
want their names
being known.

so, they're
stuck...

caught in a world
of their own
design.

too
scared

to sign
their names.

and
too proud
to
admit it.

they sent me for

x-rays
to see what's
wrong with my back.

the tech was
nice enough.

she even
helped me
tie the gown
when i was having trouble.

i guess this is what
i've got now,

poems about
doctors
and techs
who are
only too kind.

that's
too bad,
i kinda liked
that other me.

the one who

climbed ladders

and
jumped fences...

who could
get out of bed
without a sigh.

but,
that's okay,

before
you know it,

i'll get to like
this new guy, too.

life's
an art,

and
the little joke
of it
is

by
the time
you

figure that out,

you're left with
x-rays,
a bad back
and a kindly tech
tying your gown
from behind.

it was taking

too long
for him
to die,

so Lawson
put another
bullet
into him,

and
just like that

it was
over.

still
holding the gun

he
turned
to Moore
and said

"that'll be
the last
god-damned time
he ever

tells me
an ace high straight
don't
beat a flush.

quit
grinnin'
like that.

sooner
or later

your time
will come, too.

deal,
will ya!"

it's raining now...

i just got back
from picking my dog up
at the groomer's.

we came in the door,
and i took off my jacket,
while she shook off the rain.

then
we both
came down here

and i once again
started in on the poem.

she's sleeping
now...

two years old and
already a
genius.

two years old and
she knows
exactly
how
to shake off

what's
bothering
her.

i never thought i'd

end
this way.

chronic pain
24/7.

it
hurts to move, it
hurts to sit, it hurts
to breathe.

that wasn't supposed
to be me.

i expected to be
hitting my 60s
fully formed.

the crazy old guy
who hit all
the elevator buttons
and ran.

never,
no way
did i
expect

for this
to happen.

but that's
okay.

you
play the hand
you're dealt.

besides,
inside
i still am
that
guy
i wanted to become.

and
whoever's
responsible
for that other thing…

you and i
gotta talk.

the neighbor died today

cancer.

she lived
with
it

nobly

and
long.

just not
long enough.

the

geese
are loud
today.

i
hear you
calling
me,

i
think.

my car battery died and

i was
waiting for
Triple A.

i thought
i'd kill some time
by writing a bit.

nothing came,
so, i
gave it up,
did the dishes,
played with
the dog and
waited,

thinking
it's just like life,
isn't it?

you do your
thing,

then
sit around
waiting
for the truck

to take you
away.

i don't know what it was

either
the crowd was wrong,

or
i was wrong…

or both.

but,
it just
wasn't working.

i read
poem after poem.

nobody laughed…

nobody clapped…

and i couldn't blame them.

i was shit,
they were shit,
and it was all
falling apart.

the walls
stunk

and
the floor
was cracked.

when
it was over
i sold some books,
grabbed my coat
and ran.

i got in the car
and put in a cd
of me reading on another night.

that night
they got my jokes,

they
loved my poems

and
i was
handsome

and tall.
the world made sense.

but it didn't matter,
because that was then

and this is
now.

so i took out the cd
and put in one by
Hank Williams.

it was a live recording
and Hank was good.

Hank was a god
and in his entire career
he never
ever
had a bad night…

did he?

with my dearest, sincerest apologies to Janis;

i've
got
them old

401K
melt-down

blues
again,

momma!

New York just

wasn't
the same.

i remember
as a kid

everything was
gray and brown

like
the old movies,

and my uncle
had this
2nd floor
walk-up,

with a
single bulb
hanging from a wire
at the top of the stairs.

i remember the night
someone
dropped
a bag of bottles
down the steps,

and the neighbors
yelled,

and my uncle
yelled
back

and the soft
grays

and warm
browns

felt safe,

and
we lounged around
in the alleys of the universe.

no, New York's not
the same.

nothing is.

except for maybe
that old girl,
sorrow.

his wife had

left,
he
lost his
job,
and
was drinking
more than
ever.

i
swear
he looked
ten years
younger.

why i'm not Buk...

beyond
the talent, of course...

there's also this
to consider:

classical music
doesn't interest me...

i don't
duke it out
in the alley
with the boys
from the bar...

i don't even know
a single prostitute,
and

my face has yet
to really show
the ravage
of my
years.

yes,
Bukowski had it

figured out.

over the course of time
he managed to
write like
a slumming
angel,

while
looking
like
hell.

imagine
that.

she loved the literary types...

men who
used
and understood
the language of words.

this made it
all the more
disconcerting
when the latest
object of her desires
rejected
her,

saying:
"i'm not your type.

really.

you're looking for
a straight declarative,

and all i've got
to offer
is a
dangling participle."

please

don't
ask
me
to

explain.

i
don't
have
any

answers.

hell,

i
barely
understand
the

questions.

the

weeds
lie
in
piles
on
the
ground.

yes,
they
will
grow
back.

that's
what
weeds
do.

"Dear John Yamrus;

I'm
sending you this
to say that
I read your
latest poem,
and I've got to say
that even poems
about Death
are vital –
but, surely
not this!

Did you
just take
a flash fiction paragraph
& vivisect it?

Please!
Tell me
this is not poetry!"

"dear sir;
this
is
not
poetry."

if

the
books
don't
get sold,

the
poems
don't
get read.

Bukowski started his novel

Post Office
with the line:

"It began
as a mistake."

most things
(good and bad)
start that way.

like
this poem,
which had me
thinking
about
all the crap i write every night,

most of it's
not very good,
but that's the way it is.

that's the way
life is.

you get up,
go to work,
come home

and go to sleep.

and
in between
you try
desperately
to hold onto the fire.

in dog obedience class...

for once,
my little Abby
did everything right.

for once,
she didn't
bite, jump or pull.

this time
she paid attention

and sat and stayed
and came
and listened...

just like
all the other dogs.

i can't tell you how much
i hated that.

we

are the
literary fallout

from
Charles
Bukowski's
ass.

and,
for some
strange reason,

it
works.

the headline read:

*"Police Find
Four More Bodies
in Suspect's Home."*

murderers,
rapists,
killers
and thieves…

all
of them

 (in their own crazy way)

looking
for

immortality,

or
entertainment,

whichever
comes
first.

dunno

got
no answers

got
no questions

got
no whys

and
got no
wherefores

all i got
is me

me
and the
poem

and
what,

my
friend,

have
you?

my publisher just called

to say
he was going
to be gone
for a few
days.

business.

he was
gonna be hitting
some book shows,

and
doing
readings.

business
was slow,

and he's
doing everything he can
to move some
books.

that's
very good of him.

i told him
if there
was anything
i could do,
all he had to do
was ask.

he also
makes some money

as
a contractor…

renovations…

tough,
physical labor.

business
was slow there, too.

only,
this time
i didn't offer to help.

i like to
think of myself as
a good guy.

but,
even
good guys
have to know
their limits.

contrary

to
popular opinion,

the
internet

has ruined
poetry

for
the world.

it has
fooled

too many
people

into
thinking

they
can do

this.

people

often
ask me

"where do you
get your ideas
for poems?"

well,
a headline
in the paper
this morning
read:

"*Ice-skating bear kills trainer*"

it
just
doesn't

get
any better
than that.

go ahead…

this one's
on me.

knock
yourself
out.

about the author

John Yamrus has been a fixture on the poetry scene since
1970. He's published 17 volumes of poetry, 2 novels and
his poetry is widely published in magazines around the
world. His poems have been taught at both the high school
and the college level and selections of his work have been
translated into several languages, including Spanish,
Swedish, Italian, French, Japanese and Romanian. His
work has been described by the great Milner Place as "... a
blade made from smooth honest steel, with the sharpest of
edges."

also by John Yamrus

New And Selected Poems
Blue Collar
Shoot The Moon
One Step at a Time
78 RPM
Keep The Change
New And Used
Start To Finish
Someone Else's Dreams (novel)
Something
Poems
Those
Coming Home
American Night
15 Poems
Heartsongs
Lovely Youth (novel)
I Love

other publications by epic rites press

FROSTBITTEN by Mark Walton
A BELLYFUL OF ANARCHY by Rob Plath
HELLBOUND by David McLean
THE BROKEN AND THE DAMNED by Jason Hardung
DEAD RECKONING by Todd Moore
CRUDELY MISTAKEN FOR LIFE by Wolfgang
Carstens
LAUGHING AT FUNERALS by David McLean

www.epicrites.org